I am Kalei, and I live in the Hawaiian
islands. I like being with Tūtūkāne.
That's the Hawaiian word for Grandfather.

1

Tūtūkāne and I often go fishing together.
At other times, we walk slowly along the beach,
and Tūtūkāne tells me about Hawaiʻi.

"Shall I tell you about Māui and his fishing
hook?" asked Tūtūkāne one day.

"That would be great," I said.

So this is what Tūtūkāne told me.

Many, many years ago a man named Māui lived
not too far away. He was smart and helpful.

One day Māui found some bone on the beach.
He said, "I'll make a fishing hook from this bone."

Māui worked slowly and carefully on his
fishing hook. He could see that it was going to be
different from most hooks. He was excited to
think of the kind of fishing he could do with it.

4

The next morning Māui hurried to the beach to find his brothers. He asked if he could go fishing with them.

At first, his brothers didn't want him along. They were afraid he would be of no help to them.

Then Māui showed them his fishing hook.
"I think with this hook, I can help make good
things happen," he said.

So his brothers said that Māui could go with
them. They all jumped into the boat and went
out to sea.

It was a great day for fishing. The sky was
blue, with only a few white clouds. Māui had
never been happier.

But Māui's brothers were watching him.

"Why don't you put your hook into the sea?"
one asked.

"You said that you were going to make good
things happen," said the other brother.
"Where are all those fish?"

"Not here," said Māui. "We have to go out
some more."

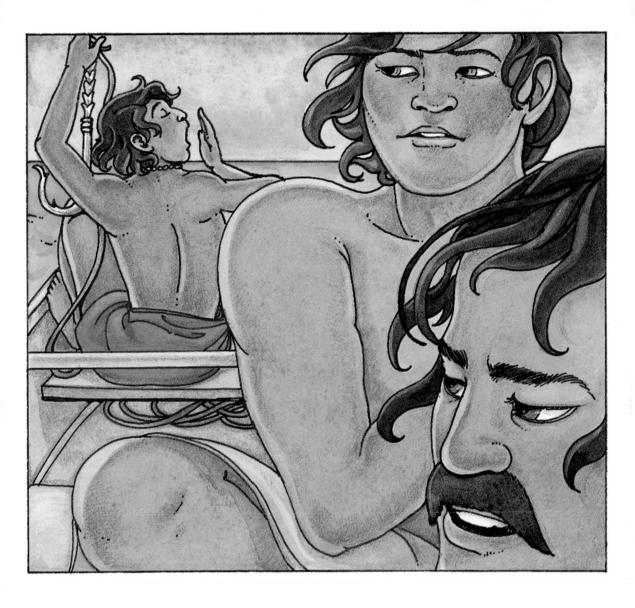

Soon the sun was overhead. The brothers were
growing even unhappier with Māui.

"Māui, when will you fish?" one said.

"We are still not out far enough," said Māui.
"We have to go out a little more."

At last Māui said, "This is far enough.
Turn around and go back home. You will know
when I get something because there will be a
great pull on the boat. But don't look back.
Just keep on going."

All at once, there was a great pull on the boat.

The brothers were very surprised.

"What does Māui have?" they asked.

But they did not turn around to look.

They pulled and pulled as they went on.

It was getting harder and harder to keep going.
"Māui, what kind of fish do you have?"
the brothers asked. "It's too big and it's getting
heavier and heavier. We can't go on much longer!"
"Don't look back," Māui said. "Keep going!"

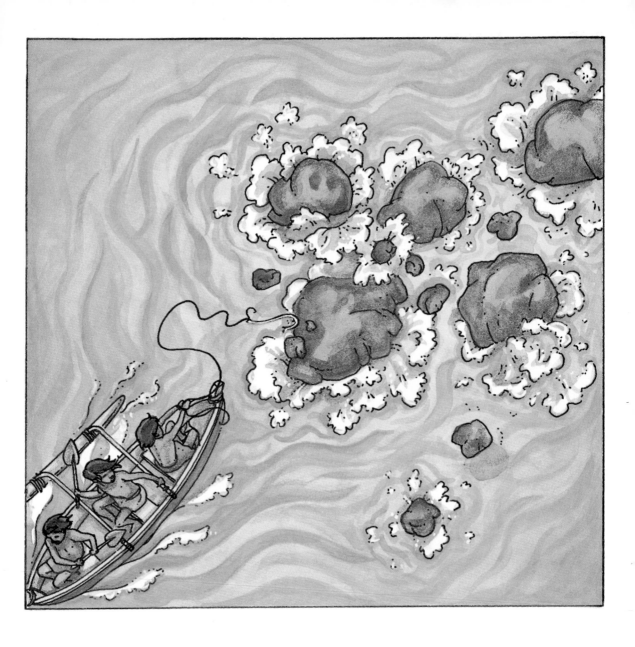

Finally one brother could stand it no longer. He stopped and turned around. Just as he turned, he saw a great mound of earth fall from Māui's hook into the sea.

"Now look what you've done!" Māui shouted.
"I was about to pull up the greatest land of all. But
you made it fall off my hook. Now all that's left are
those little islands."

14

"And that was how the Hawaiian islands
came to be," said Tūtūkāne. "The islands that
were left after Māui went fishing that day are
now our home. And I think it's the prettiest
place on earth."

"So do I," I said happily. "Thanks for telling me about our islands. Now can *we* go fishing, too?"